Mem

Inner Child

And

Letters To

Help Her Heal

Copyright

Cover designed by Jasmine Schildt

This book is a work of fiction. Names, characters, places, and incidents either are products of the author's imagination or are used fictitiously. Any resemblance to actual persons, living or dead, events, or locales is entirely coincidental.

J.N. Schildt
Visit my social networks:
www.instagram.com/lbtsurface
www.facebook.com/lbtsurface

Printed in the United States of America
ISBN-13: 978-0-578-85974-3

First Printing: February 2021
Published by Brown Sparrow Books

To all with an inner child who has yet to heal.
I hope someday you can find peace.
This one is for you

*"I don't have demons
or a dark passenger lurking inside.
Nor do I feel sorrow for no reason,
and this voice peeps out from where it hides.*

*What I have is an inner child
who has yet to heal.
Untamed and wild-
Wounds too deep to conceal."*

J.N. Schildt

Contents

PRESENT-DAY

Ever wonder
how the environment of one's upbringing
influences a person's behavior,
perspectives,
and thought process
as an adult?

People
have the impression
that once they leave the nest,
they have
this sense of freedom
and that they can escape
their childhood adversities.

For some,
they can close that door,
lock it,
and
toss the key away.

For others,
it haunts them.
It's a "ghost"
that appears in every aspect
of their lives.

I am
perpetually battling
with a ghost that creeps from my
subconscious
and into my waking world.

Sometimes,
I feel that I have forgiven those who
have hurt me;
other times,
my resentment is reawakened like a bat
out of hell.

The ramifications
that follow an adolescent
that come from a broken family
can become their shadow
as an adult.

This shadow
is not always present.
However,
when the slightest trigger
or setback
impedes their light,

it is there,
sucking the life out of them,
like bed bugs in the night.

How might one overcome
these poltergeists
that knock
one's spirit to the ground
and regenerates itself
into this heaping mess
of a human being?

I succumb
to the beauty of this world
and engulf myself
with the unconditional love
of my family.

But wait…
the euphoria dispels
just as soon as it arrives.

This feeling
is all too familiar,
and I find comfort in it

despite
the pain it possesses.

I surrender
to the lingering pain
that creates a heavy feeling
in my chest
as if I am suffocating,
and I
have the weight of the world
on my shoulders.

It is a never-ending cycle.
I am but a prisoner in my own mind.

THE BEGINNING

She can't pretend
that she isn't bothered
when they make her feel less than...

Not with so many words,
but through evidence
that she painfully observes.

But is her reality real?
Does her lack of self-esteem
impact how she truly feels?

Memories
can be distant;
like peeking through
the morning fog.
Trying to make
out what it is
that's on the
other side.

But it's too thick.
So, you're forced to
stitch together
bits and pieces to create
a feeling to accompany it.

This is where I began to live inside my head!

Dear inner child,

Truth is…
your reality is no more
real than theirs.
Everyone's reality is real;
However, it's how one's mind
perceive and interpret the events
that makes it different.

Perhaps we can take a walk down
memory lane.
Together, we can figure out where it
all went wrong.
Together, we can change our narrative.
Together we can heal.

I was
the second
child.

My mother
was no longer
a first time
mom.

Often
the "first" of
EVERYTHING
is exciting!

But…
I was the
second
child;

Less
excitement,
less
attention,
less
photos,
and less
love to give.

Less of everything!

Inner child,

Being the second child
is a blessing.
Before you were born
you already had a friend waiting-
your sibling.

I know that it may appear
that you are less than.
But my dear,
you are more than
what you deem
to be true.
Your low self-esteem
is playing tricks on you.

You must learn to understand your
worth. Don't allow the lack of attention
from others to dictate your place on this
earth. You may be the second-born;
however, you are also a miracle placed
on this earth. You were not placed here
by accident. You have strength! You outpaced the
rest of those wishing to come into this world.
That's a testament to how truly special you are!

My mother
was a work-a-holic.
So, I never
really saw her.

Or is it
because I can't
remember
spending time
with her
that makes me
think that I
never really saw her?

I was jealous of other kids with doting mothers.

Inner child,

Just because she
wasn't always there-
That doesn't mean she didn't care.
I know sometimes it can be rough.
You crave for affection; it can be tough.

But I hope you can see.
That nothing in this world is for free.
Perhaps, that's why she was always
working.
To afford those barbies and dolls
you loved collecting.

Let's chalk it up to that.
Even if it isn't a fact.
Though, it makes a lot of sense.
Let's go with that pretense.

Looking at things from different perspectives
is a splendid approach in dealing with your
mind from running away with personal and
bias opinions.

My father
had a
TERRIBLE
temper.

He brought
home his
frustrations
from work.

*Perhaps that's why my mother was
a work-a-holic?*

Inner child,

I am sorry you had to witness anger
at a very young age-
I wish he didn't have so much rage!
His displaced anger was quite ugly.
People don't realize how destructive
they can be.
Until finally,
They've lost everything due to their
misery.

Just remember… storms don't last
forever-
You are a resilient child!
Find solitude within yourself.
There you'll find a place to escape
when the outside world becomes
too chaotic.

I
have
ALWAYS
been
a
sensitive child.

Too sensitive!

My brother
was the
opposite.

I never really
knew him.
I avoided him
to prevent
from getting my
feelings hurt.

The irony
is that,
we are so much
alike
in so many ways.

This is where I began to avoid people.

Inner child,

Sometimes, people are misunderstood.
Deep down inside he is truly good.
You were both cut from the
same cloth,
There is gentleness under all his silence
and angry froth.

Avoiding people doesn't sound so bad.
I know you do it to avoid getting hurt and
from feeling sad.
So, I understand!
Just please don't hide your head in the sand.

You need to learn to deal with unpleasantness;
Sweeping things under the rug won't let you rest.
It will only marinade and fester,
instead of making things better.

If you avoid everyone,
you'll be all alone and missing out
on what could be fun.

When my parents
used to quarrel,
I would lay in
my bed
and
pray for them
to get
DIVORCED.

God answered my prayers at the cost of
losing my sanity.

Inner child,

It's not your fault,
that your parent's marriage came to
a halt.
The only prayer God answered,
was to ensure that you were heard.

What ensued was not to punish you.
Your parents were supposed to ensure
your security too.
You and your brother were supposed to be-
their number one priority.

Instead, they got it all wrong.
They failed to make you feel like you still
belonged.
In the future, they'll atone for their mistakes.
Have an open heart for the future's sake.

God works in mysterious ways.
You wouldn't be where you are today-
If it weren't for the trials and tribulations
set forth.
So, don't lose hope; in due time you'll find
your support.

THE DIVORCE

When my father
moved out,
he left the door
wide open.

My mother trailed
him,
but walked
a different path.

I guess she got lost
because for a while she never came back.

Inner child,

*I wish I could come up with an excuse
to change this story.
But I just can't come up with any, I am
truly sorry.*

*I am sure it kept them up at night.
Though, it still doesn't make it right-
At least, your mother came back.
Her priority fell through the cracks.*

*I wish that I could just pick you up
and whisk you away from the hurt
and confusion that you must feel.
It is one thing to experience a family
breaking up. However, to have to go
through it alone can be so detrimental
to any child. Not everyone understands
how to be a good parent. People have
different expectations and different
definitions of what it means to be a
parent.*

I waited
for either one
to come back.

I cleaned
the entire house
hoping that
a cleaner
house would
make them want
to come home.

I waited...

But they never did
and I was forced
to live with my aunt
and my brother
lived
with another.

*It was then that I no longer felt like
I had a home.*

Home is not a place
  It is a feeling

And I was homesick!

My family no longer exists

I felt
Forgotten
l**O**st
dese**R**ted
Sad
Alone
bro**K**en
Empty
Neglected

I felt forsaken!

I felt
UNWANTED!

I felt
that I
was
NOT ENOUGH!

*Now I need affirmation
to feel loved.*

Inner child,

Life can be so unkind.
It impacts our minds
in a negative way.
Not sure why it was hard for your mom to stay.

Child you were never alone!
But how could you have known?
Your mother left you with her family-
Until she could get her life together, can't you see?

It was the only way she knew how to survive,
from the problems she had, although it wasn't right.
She was selfish!
But it made you grow up to be a doting mom that's
selfless.

I know the feeling of being abandoned still haunts you.
You still feel the emptiness and loneliness that ensued.
But these are things we can work on... together!
We need to retrain your brain to help make you feel better.

Finally,
my mother
came back
for me
and
I was excited!

I would feel
whole
again.

I would feel
at home
again.

A
place where
I belonged.

But
my new
"home"
was where she was
all along-
when I needed her the most!

New is not always welcomed.

New beginnings
usually mean
carving a new path.

A second chance!

But I was a
wounded child;
Too hurt
to see past my pain.

I became a prisoner in my own mind.

Inner child,

Depression is so ugly!
It's hard to clearly see.
It's difficult to think with an unclear mind.
It's difficult to leave the past behind!
Where it belongs.
Instead, we dwell on things that have gone wrong.

Truthfully, I still struggle with this one.
Depression isn't curable; however, it is
treatable. We can learn to lessen the pain,
how to distract ourselves when the feeling
of loneliness overcomes us once again. We
can venture back into the past and stitch
together a new narrative to help cope with
the emotional pain that comes with specific
memories. We can learn to see things from
different perspectives. We just need to have the
will and the patience to help ourselves. You'll
get there! You'll see! Through a good therapist,
they can help with psychotherapy.

I used to play
in my grandmother's
room.

On top of her
dresser,
she had photos
of all her
grandchildren
EXCEPT
mine.

Perhaps she
forgot?
or
she was still
getting to
it?

*The feeling of inadequacy overcame
me once more.*

Inner child,

I just want to give you a warm hug.
These are some of those feelings that shouldn't
be swept under the rug.
You no longer have any confidence-
and it's messing with your head at your heart's expense.

You know she loved you dearly,
She was probably still working on your photo, can't
you see?
She was always warm and kind.
An amazing grandmother; she was one of a kind.

Yes, your picture was not there.
No, it wasn't because she didn't care!
It's not uncommon to forget.
You know how old people can get.

Sometimes we only see what we want to see.
When our mind starts playing tricks with our memories.
Unfortunately,
we can be our worst enemy.

There is always an explanation why things happen.
Our brain tends to distort the facts
when our self-esteem is low.
Our mind takes us to the worst possible thoughts
and scenarios.

Every time
I saw my father
he would take
me shopping.

During special occasions
he would swing by
to give me a
card
with money
to spend.

But...all I wanted was to spend quality time with him.

Inner child,

I know you missed your dad.
It's hard to be away from a parent-it's sad!
He was trying to make up for being away,
by taking you shopping and showering you
with gifts because he knew he couldn't stay.

For some, this is the only way they know how,
to show their love and be present in your life
somehow.
I know it wasn't precisely what you wanted.
At least he was there and didn't completely
take you for granted.

Some kids aren't as lucky,
to still have a father in their lives, can't you see?
Let's always look at the bright side;
A lot of the times, it can trump the negative feelings
we harbor inside.

JUNIOR HIGH

Making friends
was difficult.
I never felt
like I
belonged.

I wore
sweaters
and jackets
in 90 degree
weather
for security.

Without it,
I felt exposed
as if others
could see me
and
all my insecurities.

I liked
feeling invisible,
hidden,
blending in with the
background.

I was a loner and developed social anxiety.

The library
was my sanctuary.

It was my go-to
during
recess
and
lunch break.

I began to withdraw from others.

Inner child,

Even though you try to hide- I can see you!
I see a smart, caring, and special person...it's true!
Under all that armor and shield,
lives an exceptional girl that's concealed.

It's okay to feel like you don't belong.
There really isn't anything wrong!
Some people are created differently;
People have different interests and would
rather be free-
Than to conform to what everyone is doing.
Being someone you're not, can be exhausting.

Just remember you are beautiful inside and out!
You're just more reserved,
being in the spotlight is not what you're about.
I just wish you wouldn't try to hide-
so that others can see your beauty inside.
You are unique; you are rare; you are one of a kind!
No one can compare! You think and feel deeply; you
have an intricate and beautiful mind.

Trigger Warning!

Within the next few pages,
self-harm is discussed.

The
emotional pain
didn't stop.

It dug deeper
and found itself
burrowed
DEEP
in
my mind
nestled
within my soul.

Forlorn to escape.

I learned to lessen the pain by bleeding it out.

Sometimes…
I stare into nothing-
and imagine myself laying bare in a
field of flowers.
Curled into a ball screaming and wailing
under heavenly bowers.

Angels weeping.
Their tears they scour-
Showering and cleansing
this ailing that devours
my mind that's decaying
from evils insatiable powers.

I scream at the gods crying-
Blaming, pointing fingers for hours.
Alas, I jump on to my knees praying
till this detrimental mind finally
cowers.

I snap back into reality pretending
to be this beautiful creature that
flowers.
In a world filled with illusions of
people smiling
behind their mask with each encounter.

I
hid my razor
the way an
addict
hid their drugs.

When the
emotional pain was
too much
to bear.

I cut to release
the pain.

*The physical pain hurt less, and I gladly exchanged
one for the other.*

Inner child,

I wish that I could step into a time machine.
I would transport myself to right before you became
a teen.
Teach you ways to deal with the pain,
instead of resorting to self-harm and redirect
the blame.

This is so common amongst young children.
My heart aches when I hear about it again and again.
You shouldn't exchange one pain for another.
It doesn't help you get any better.

Instead, it makes things worse.
I would rather you find another way before you end
up in a hearse.
I know you self-harm not only to lessen the emotional
and mental pain.
But, you are also punishing yourself because you hate
who you've become along with your tormented brain.

But dear child you NEED to learn to love YOU!
Find other ways to cope with your pain; there are
lots of things that you can do.

Let's start by writing a list of positive things of
yourself.
Read it every day, then store it on your shelf.
For safekeeping;
You'll know where to find it when you need it
again, and while you're weeping.

Because you know it will happen-
You can start by first being your own friend.
Give yourself pep talks.
Find safe places to go on walks.

Get some kisses from the sun.
Maybe even go for a run.
Release those happy chemicals naturally;
It will help you feel better, you will see!

Play your favorite song and turn up the sound,
Dance to your heart's content, it can drown-
out those pesky voices inside your head.
Music can be therapeutic, go ahead listen, and
bob your head.

Get into the rhythm and move your body.
Let's get the blood flowing so you can
feel a little less sad and little more happy!

My mind,
a battlefield.
Crumbled walls-
and pierced shields.

A warzone where sanity-
collides with insanity.
Where rage and sorrow dance-
to a forlorn rhythmic trance.

It is not beautiful,
aesthetic,
or poetry.
It is irrational,
unapologetic,
and guilt-ridden ugly.

My mind.
A battlefield.
I, a ghost,
should I yield.
But not today!
Or any other day.

I am here
to stay.
For I am a fighter!
A warrior-

A strong willed
SURVIVOR!

My inner child
is at it again.
Resurfacing from
its repressed den.

Screaming
and whimpering
relentlessly trying-
Coercing me
to feel her sorrow.
Past and present
muffled tomorrow.

After all this time,
she has yet to heal.
My inner child
forlorn from
her ordeal.
Slowly inhale,
hold 1-2-3.
Gradually release,
1-2-3.

Do it again, repeat
until she's lulled back
to sleep.

Thank you for your interest in Memories Of My Inner Child And Letters To Help Her Heal. If you enjoyed what you have read, please follow J.N. Schildt and stay tuned for Part 2 of this collection. Please don't forget to leave a review and help J.N. Schildt reach others who could benefit from this chapbook.

Memories Of My Inner Child

Made in the USA
Las Vegas, NV
12 January 2022